Steve

Reich

Nagoya Marimbas

for Two Marimbas

Full Score

BOOSEY &HAWKES

AN IMAGEM COMPANY

DISTRIBUTED BY

HAL•LEONARD®
CORPORATION
7777 W. BLUEMOUND RD. P.O. BOX 13819 MILWAUKEE, WI 53213

HENDON MUSIC

Commissioned by Sekar Sakura, Nagoya College of Music,
in honor of the opening of Shirakawa Hall

First performed 21 December 1994 at Shirakawa Hall, Nagoya City, Japan
by Sekar Sakura, Yukie Kurihara and Maki Kurihara, marimbas

duration: ca. 5 minutes

Steve

Reich

Nagoya
Marimbas

for Two Marimbas

Marimba 1

BOOSEY & HAWKES

AN IMAGEM COMPANY

DISTRIBUTED BY

HAL•LEONARD®
CORPORATION
7777 W. BLUEMOUND RD. P.O. BOX 13819 MILWAUKEE, WI 53213

HENDON MUSIC

NAGOYA MARIMBAS

Marimba 1

STEVE REICH
(1994)

*Crescendi and decrescendi over repeated measures last for the duration of the complete repetition.

Printed in U.S.A. 1998

Steve

Reich

Nagoya
Marimbas

for Two Marimbas

Marimba 2

BOOSEY & HAWKES

AN IMAGEM COMPANY

DISTRIBUTED BY
HAL•LEONARD®
CORPORATION
7777 W. BLUEMOUND RD. P.O. BOX 13819 MILWAKEE, WI 53213

HENDON MUSIC

NAGOYA MARIMBAS

Marimba 2

STEVE REICH
(1994)

*Crescendi and decrescendi over repeated measures last for the duration of the complete repetition.

PEB11

Printed in U.S.A. 1998

NAGOYA MARIMBAS

Steve Reich
(1994)

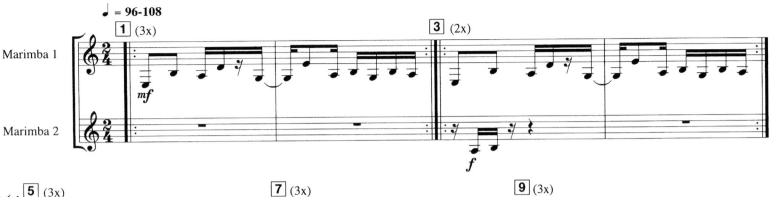

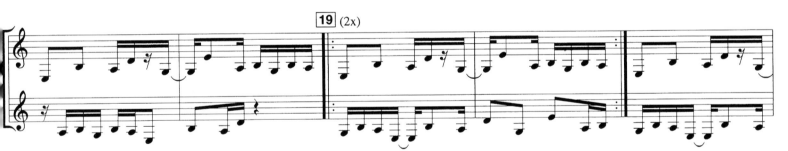

PEB11

Printed in U.S.A. 1998

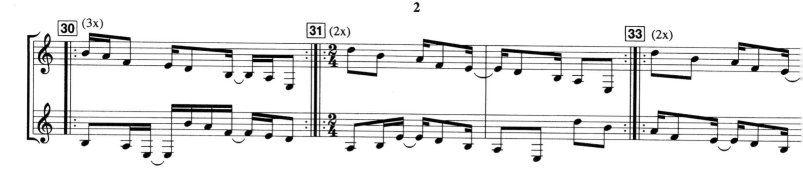

*Crescendi and decrescendi over repeated measures last for the duration of the complete repetition.

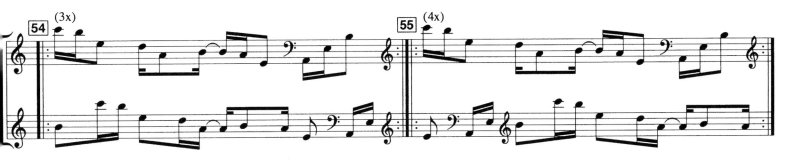